CLASSICAL COMPOSERS

Pyotr Ilyich TCHAIKOVSKY

by Joanne Mattern
with Consultation by John Viscardi,
Executive Director of Classic Lyric Arts
illustrated by Marilena Perilli

RED CHAIR PRESS

Egremont, Massachusetts

Classical Composers has been produced and published by Red Chair Press Books for Young Readers:
Red Chair Press LLC   PO Box 333   South Egremont, MA 01258
www.redchairpress.com

 Download a Free Activity Guide on our website.

For more information about Classic Lyric Arts, visit www.classiclyricarts.org.

Names: Mattern, Joanne, 1963- author. | Viscardi, John, consultant. | Perilli, Marilena, illustrator.

Title: Pyotr Ilyich Tchaikovsky / by Joanne Mattern, with consultation by John Viscardi, executive director of Classic Lyric Arts ; illustrated by Marilena Perilli.

Description: Egremont, Massachusetts : Red Chair Press, [2025] | Series: Classical composers | Interest age level: 007-010. | Includes bibliographical references and index. | Summary: Pyotr Ilyich Tchaikovsky (1840–1893), a Russian composer, created some of the most beloved classical music of the Romantic era ... Colorful illustrations plus photographs of meaningful sites and settings connect readers to important points in Tchaikovsky's history. A timeline and B Sharp sidebars add details to the composer's life story.--Publisher.

Identifiers: ISBN: 978-1-64371-442-4 (LB hardcover) | 978-1-64371-443-1 (paperback) | 978-1-64371-445-5 (S&L ebook) | LCCN: 2024936083

Subjects: LCSH: Tchaikovsky, Peter Ilich, 1840-1893--Juvenile literature. | Composers--Russia--Biography--Juvenile literature. | CYAC: Tchaikovsky, Peter Ilich, 1840-1893. | Composers--Russia--Biography. | LCGFT: Biographies. | BISAC: JUVENILE NONFICTION / Biography & Autobiography / Music. | JUVENILE NONFICTION / Biography & Autobiography / Performing Arts. | JUVENILE NONFICTION / Music / Classical.

Classification: LCC: ML410.C4 M38 2025 | DDC: 780.92--dc23

Copyright © 2026 Red Chair Press LLC
RED CHAIR PRESS, the RED CHAIR and associated logos are
registered trademarks of Red Chair Press LLC.

All rights reserved. No part of this book may be reproduced, stored in an information or retrieval system, or transmitted in any form by any means, electronic, mechanical including photocopying, recording, or otherwise without the prior written permission from the Publisher. For permissions, contact info@redchairpress.com

Image credits: Cover, 4, 6, 11, 12, 20, 24, 26, 29, 31 © Shutterstock; p. 4 © Bridgeman Images; pp. 12, 21, 24 © Lebrecht Music Arts/Bridgeman Images; p. 25 © Michael Dwyer/AP Images.

Illustrations: Marilena Perilli, except p. 7 by Joe LeMonnier

Printed in the United States of America

0425 1P CGF25

Table of Contents

Playing Music for Fun 4
A Change of Heart 12
A Generous Friend 20
Cannons and Nutcrackers 24
Timeline 30
Glossary 32
Read More 32
Index 32

Playing Music for Fun

Pyotr Ilyich Tchaikovsky (PYOH-ter uhl-YEECH chy-KAAF-skee) is Russia's most famous **composer**. He created some of the most beautiful music in the world. The music he wrote for **ballets** is enjoyed today as some of the most widely performed. But when he was growing up, no one expected Tchaikovsky to become a great composer.

Pyotr Ilyich Tchaikovsky was born on May 7, 1840. He was born in Votkinsk, Russia. Pyotr's father worked as a manager in the mines. His mother cared for Pyotr and his brothers and sisters.

Pyotr began taking piano lessons when he was about four years old. He enjoyed playing the piano. But it was just a hobby for the little boy and his family.

The Pyotr Tchaikovsky Museum is in the city of Votkinsk, Russia, where Pyotr spent his childhood.

One day, Pyotr's father brought home a new musical instrument. It was called an orchestrion. The orchestrion could make the sounds of several different musical instruments. Pyotr loved this new instrument. He tried to copy the music it played by playing the piano.

The orchestrion inspired Pyotr to start writing music. He wrote his first **composition** when he was just four years old. His sister helped him write the song.

B♯ B SHARP: Pyotr was very sensitive. At school, he often cried if he made a mistake or if his teacher scolded him.

Pyotr's family could tell he truly loved music. But people in Russia at that time did not think composing music was an important job. No one even thought about sending Pyotr to school to learn about music.

Instead, Pyotr's family sent him to a boarding school when he was nine years old. The school was in the grand city of St. Petersburg. Pyotr spent nine years at the all-boys school where he had many close friends. Pyotr's parents wanted him to be a lawyer. Pyotr studied history, politics, and law. He was a great student at everything he studied.

A Change of Heart

Pyotr studied hard in school. But he missed playing music. He began taking piano lessons in private. His teacher Luigi Piccioli thought Pyotr was an excellent musician. He helped Pyotr learn about Italian music, which had more melody than the German classical music popular in Russia.

In 1859, Pyotr got a job with the Russian government. He worked as a **clerk** for the Ministry of Justice. Pyotr worked as a clerk for four years. But soon he felt bored working in an office all day.

The Italian instructor Luigi Piccioli was the first person to fully recognize and encourage Pyotr's musical talents.

In 1862, a music school opened in St. Petersburg. It was called the St. Petersburg **Conservatory**. Pyotr took many classes there. He learned about all different kinds of music. He learned about composition too. His teachers **encouraged** him and told him he was good at writing music. Soon, music was all Pyotr could think about.

In 1865, something exciting happened to Tchaikovsky. One of his original compositions was performed in public for the first time. A famous composer named Johann Strauss II **conducted** Tchaikovsky's *Characteristic Dances* at a concert in St. Petersburg.

Tchaikovsky graduated from the conservatory in 1865. Then he moved to Moscow and got a job at a music school. He continued to write music and also conducted concerts.

A photo of Tchaikovsky taken in Berlin in 1893 shows him holding his head.

Tchaikovsky did not really like being a teacher. What he liked more was composing. Over the next few years, he wrote several operas. He wrote **symphonies** and **string quartets** too. In 1868, he wrote his first **opera**, *The Voyevoda*.

People in Russia began noticing this young composer. They liked his music. It was full of different emotions. Some of Tchaikovsky's music made people feel sad. Some of his music made them happy.

B♯ B SHARP: Tchaikovsky often included tunes from Russian folk songs within his music.

A Generous Friend

In 1875, Tchaikovsky traveled to Europe. He visited many different countries where music was highly valued. He enjoyed going to the opera and going to concerts. Tchaikovsky's trip to Europe gave him lots of new ideas.

In 1876, Tchaikovsky wrote his first ballet. It was called *Swan Lake*. However, most people did not like it. They said the music was too noisy and loud and took attention away from the dancers.

Tchaikovsky felt bad when people did not like his music. But those feelings did not stop him from composing more music.

Tchaikovsky's *Swan Lake* had its premier or first public performance in 1877 in Moscow, Russia. Polina Karpakova danced the lead role.

In 1876, Tchaikovsky got a letter from Nadezhda von Meck. Von Meck had a lot of money. She liked Tchaikovsky's work and wanted to help him. Von Meck became Tchaikovsky's **patron**. She gave him an allowance every year. This money meant that Tchaikovsky could quit his job. Now he could afford to compose music all the time.

B# **B SHARP:** Tchaikovsky and von Meck became good friends. They wrote 1,200 letters to each other over the next 14 years. But they only met once!

In his last letter to von Meck, Pyotr wrote: "...you probably yourself do not suspect the fullness of your good deed!"
source: Tchaikovsky Museum

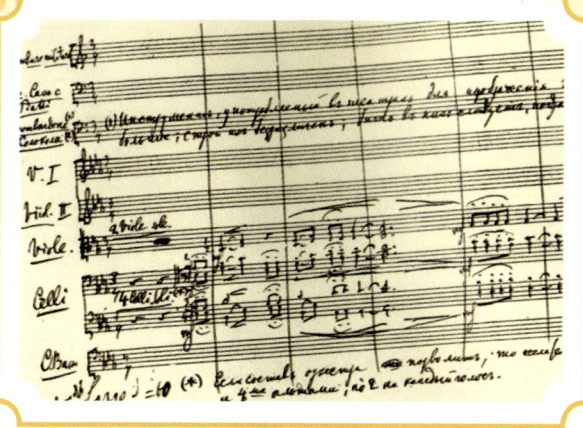

Cannons and Nutcrackers

Over the next 15 years, Tchaikovsky wrote his most famous music. One of his most dramatic pieces was the *1812 Overture*. In 1812, French general Napoleon Bonaparte tried to invade Russia. Russia won the battle. The *1812 Overture* celebrates this victory. The music is loud and dramatic. Church bells ring as part of the performance. There are even blasts from cannons!

B♯ **B SHARP:** The *1812 Overture* is often played at Fourth of July concerts in the United States, complete with the boom from fireworks.

The Nutcracker ballet is popular during the Christmas holidays. Here it is performed in 2012 by the Children's Ballet Theatre of Moscow.

In 1890, Tchaikovsky wrote a ballet called *Sleeping Beauty. Sleeping Beauty* was very popular with audiences. A theater director asked Tchaikovsky to write another ballet.

Tchaikovsky had read a short story called "The Nutcracker and the Mouse King." He used this as the inspiration to write his ballet, *The Nutcracker.* In it, Tchaikovsky tells the story of a young girl who visits a magical fantasy world on Christmas Eve.

At first, people did not like *The Nutcracker.* However, this ballet went on to become one of Tchaikovsky's most famous and popular works. Today, seeing the ballet is a Christmas tradition around the world.

Between 1890 and 1893, Tchaikovsky traveled all around the world. Audiences in Europe and the United States loved watching him conduct his music.

In October 1893, Tchaikovsky conducted his new *Sixth Symphony* in St. Petersburg. A few days later, he got sick with a disease called **cholera**. Tchaikovsky died on November 6. He was 53 years old.

Pyotr Ilyich Tchaikovsky wrote 169 compositions during his life. People today enjoy his ballets, symphonies, and other pieces. His music is well-known around the world. Tchaikovsky's dramatic music is beautiful to listen to.

B♯   B SHARP: The Sixth Symphony is now called *Pathétique*, meaning emotional, and is thought to have been his favorite composition.

Tchaikovsky's grave in St. Petersburg, Russia.

Important Dates in Pyotr Ilyich Tchaikovsky's Life

1840   Pyotr Ilyich Tchaikovsky is born in Votkinsk, Russia.

1845   Tchaikovsky begins taking piano lessons.

1849   Tchaikovsky attends boarding school and studies to become a lawyer.

1859   Tchaikovsky begins working as a clerk for the Ministry of Justice.

1862   Tchaikovsky begins taking classes at the St. Petersburg Conservatory.

1863   Tchaikovsky quits his job as a law clerk.

1875   Tchaikovsky writes his first ballet, *Swan Lake*.

1876   A wealthy woman becomes Tchaikovsky's sponsor.

1890   Tchaikovsky writes the ballet *Sleeping Beauty*.

1892   Tchaikovsky writes the ballet *The Nutcracker*.

1893   Tchaikovsky dies in St. Petersburg on November 6 only a few days after first conducting his final *Sixth Symphony*.

Glossary

ballets dramatic, story-telling dances performed to music

cholera a serious disease caused by drinking dirty or unclean water

clerk a person who keeps records in an office

composer a person who writes music

composition a written work of music

conducted led the musicians of an orchestra or chorus

conservatory a school for studying music

encouraged spoke positively to someone about something

opera a dramatic work set to music for singers and an orchestra

patron a person who supports an artist by giving him or her money to live on

string quartets musical groups that include four stringed instruments

symphonies long pieces of music for an orchestra

Read More About Tchaikovsky

Venezia, Mike. *Peter Tchaikovsky*. Scholastic, 2018.

Warner-Reed, Emma. *Tchaikovsky* (Classical Giants). Calendar House Press, 2024.

Index

Bonaparte, Napoleon 24
cholera 28
Moscow 16, 21
Nutcracker, The 26–27
orchestrion 9
Overture, 1812 24
Piccioli, Luigi 12–13
Russia, Votkinsk 6
Sleeping Beauty 27
St. Petersburg 11, 15, 16, 28, 29
Strauss II, Johann 16
Swan Lake 20–21
von Meck, Nadezhda 22–23
Voyevoda, The 19

Sculpture of Pyotr Ilyich Tchaikovsky in a museum park, in Klin, Russia near Moscow. The museum's Summer house is where he wrote much of his music.